WORKBOOK FOR THE HEAT WILL KILL YOU FIRST

(A Guide to Jeff Goodell's Book)

The Effective Guide to Preserving our Planet from Adverse Climate Change and other Destroying Factors

HOW TO USE THIS WORKBOOK

- Have a deep and sincere desire to do the things that is recommended here.

- Ponder upon and meditate on the food for thought, reflecting on how they relate to you, what you're advised to do and how to go about doing them.

- In the note section, write down important decisions you've made, relating to the things you've learnt.

- Don't discard this book when you're done with the 7 – Days Program. Instead, always have it in mind, never failing to return when you appear to be deviating.

- Make this a lifestyle. You'd find out that there was far more to gain in the main book through using this practical guide.

- Never assume that the lessons here are difficult and impossible to achieve, they're realistic and made easy for you.

- Follow the daily outline religiously, don't jump days or prioritize one activity over the other.

- Everything outlined here is important for you, don't neglect any.

- We recommend that you spread love and help with this workbook, give people whom you feel would need it. It could go a long way.

ALL THE BEST AS YOU VENTURE INTO THIS.....

1ˢᵗ DAY

FOOD FOR THOUGHT

Following the three "R's" has been a highly effective way of battling climate change for decades. They stand for **Reduce, Reuse, Recycle.**

TASK FOR THIS DAY

Cut down on the things you throw away, learn to start reusing or recycling products to save this planet.

KEEP THIS TO HEART...

When you uphold the 3 R's, a great deal of our planet will be saved.

IMPORTANT REFLECTIONS (NOTES)

_____
_____
_____
_____
_____
_____
_____
_____
_____
_____
_____
_____

———————

PIN THIS!

Always remember to reduce, reuse and recycle.

2nd DAY

FOOD FOR THOUGHT

Every person has the chance to volunteer for cleanups and humanitarian activities that'd save the planet.

TASK FOR THIS DAY

Choose something out of your free will to be doing for this planet in order to save it from your own quota.

KEEP THIS TO HEART...

If everyone volunteers to carry out activities that'd save this earth, the bulk of the whole thing would be saved.

IMPORTANT REFLECTIONS (NOTES)

_____

_____

_____

_____

_____

_____

_____

_____

_____

_____

PIN THIS!

What have you chosen to do for our world?

3rd DAY

FOOD FOR THOUGHT

Education has always been key and is still key up till today. Understand that enlightening people makes the work easier for you.

TASK FOR THIS DAY

Research more on climate change and preserving this planet in order to be able to enlighten others.

KEEP THIS TO HEART...

When people are enlightened, they work towards the given goal.

IMPORTANT REFLECTIONS (NOTES)

_____

_____

_____

_____

_____

_____

_____

_____

_____

_____

PIN THIS!

Education makes everything better.

4th DAY

FOOD FOR THOUGHT

Shopping wisely has its way of saving our planet. You need to be particular at buying reusable items.

TASK FOR THIS DAY

Buy less plastic and more of reusuable bags. Reduce how you purchase items that are not biodegradable.

KEEP THIS TO HEART...

Some products are not capable of being disposed, they end up polluting the place.

IMPORTANT REFLECTIONS (NOTES)

_____

_____

_____

_____

_____

_____

_____

_____

_____

_____

_____

_____

_____

_____

PIN THIS!

Biodegradable items are the best option.

5th DAY

FOOD FOR THOUGHT

Greenhouse gas emissions have long been one of the major causes of climate change.

TASK FOR THIS DAY

Start using long-lasting light bulbs, solar and other equipment that do not produce gas emissions.

KEEP THIS TO HEART...

Simple practices like turning off the light bulb when not in use saves the earth.

IMPORTANT REFLECTIONS (NOTES)

_____

_____

_____

_____

_____

_____

_____

_____

_____

_____

_____

_____

PIN THIS!

Don't compromise or neglect excessive gas emissions.

6th DAY

FOOD FOR THOUGHT

Trees have been recognized to possess highly therapeutic impact on our climate.

TASK FOR THIS DAY

Plant a tree today to save our planet tomorrow. Don't hesitate to do this.

KEEP THIS TO HEART...

Trees provide oxygen and food, they equally save energy and clean the air.

IMPORTANT REFLECTIONS (NOTES)

PIN THIS!

Trees are good for this earth.

7th DAY

FOOD FOR THOUGHT

Sending untreated chemicals into our waterways is a sure way of destroying this planet. Know this today.

TASK FOR THIS DAY

Endeavor to treat every chemical into less harmful substances before sending them into the waterways. All possible means to reduce waste chemicals should be implemented.

KEEP THIS TO HEART...

Those chemicals poison the water, kill aquatic organisms and pollute the atmosphere.

IMPORTANT REFLECTIONS (NOTES)

PIN THIS!

Stop indiscriminate dumping of chemicals and refuse into the sea.

CONGRATULATIONS!

YOU MADE IT TO THE END OF THE 7 DAYS PROGRAM.

IMBIBE THE THINGS YOU'VE LEARNT AS A LIFESTYLE!

Made in the USA
Middletown, DE
26 August 2023